Faith Is

Written by Kathleen Gwilliam

Illustrated by Danika Runyan

CFI • An imprint of Cedar Fort, Inc.
Springville, Utah

FAITH IS believing
in God up above,

that He is your father
and has perfect love.

FAITH IS trusting that
Christ is your Savior,
that His Atonement and
love will not waiver.

FAITH IS relying on
the Holy Ghost,
believing He'll guide you
when needed the most.

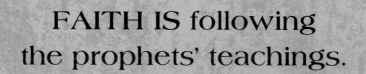

FAITH IS following
the prophets' teachings.

Trusting Christ leads
them in what they
are preaching.

FAITH IS still hoping for
things you can't see,

like sealing together
your whole family tree.

FAITH IS believing that
God answers prayers;
trusting He's listening,
and that He cares.

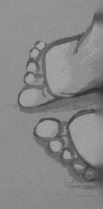

FAITH IS doing
what God asks
of you,
showing obedience
in all that you do.

FAITH IS acknowledging
blessings that come

and understanding who
your gifts are from.

Acting in FAITH IS a
choice you can choose
through thoughts, deeds,
behaviors, and words that you use.

Miracles happen when
using FAITH'S power.
Doubt, fear, and heartache
your faith can devour.

FAITH gives you courage
to conquer temptation.

FAITH based in Christ
is the way to salvation.

FAITH will develop
the more that you use it.
God strengthens FAITH
as you actively choose it.

Read scriptures, say prayers, let your gratitude show.

Keep commandments,
try hard, and your
FAITH, it will grow!

Yes, FAITH is believing,
hoping, and doing;
following Christ, fully
trusting, and choosing.

BELIEVING IN GOD: Mosiah 4:9

9 Believe in God; believe that he is, and that he created all things, both in heaven and in earth; believe that he has all wisdom, and all power, both in heaven and in earth; believe that man doth not comprehend all the things which the Lord can comprehend.

TRUSTING: Doctrine and Covenants 11:12

12 And now, verily, verily, I say unto thee, put your trust in that spirit which leadeth to do good—yea, to do justly, to walk humbly, to judge righteously; and this is my Spirit.

RELYING ON THE HOLY GHOST: 2 Nephi 32:5

5 For behold, again I say unto you that if ye will enter in by the way, and receive the Holy Ghost, it will show unto you all things what ye should do.

FOLLOWING THE PROPHET: 1 Nephi 22:2

2 And I, Nephi, said unto them: Behold they were manifest unto the prophet by the voice of the Spirit; for by the Spirit are all things made known unto the prophets, which shall come upon the children of men according to the flesh.

HOPING: Alma 32:21

21 And now as I said concerning faith—faith is not to have a perfect knowledge of things; therefore if ye have faith ye hope for things which are not seen, which are true.

BELIEVING IN PRAYER: Doctrine and Covenants 112:10

10 Be thou humble; and the Lord thy God shall lead thee by the hand, and give thee answer to thy prayers.

DOING: James 2:17–18

17 Even so faith, if it hath not works, is dead, being alone.

18 Yea, a man may say, Thou hast faith, and I have works: shew me thy faith without thy works, and I will shew thee my faith by my works.

ACKNOWLEDGING: Proverbs 3:5–6

5 Trust in the Lord with all thine heart; and lean not unto thine own understanding.

6 In all thy ways acknowledge him, and he shall direct thy paths.

MIRACLES THROUGH FAITH: James 5:15

15 And the prayer of faith shall save the sick, and the Lord shall raise him up; and if he have committed sins, they shall be forgiven him.

SALVATION THROUGH FAITH: Mosiah 3:9

9 And lo, he cometh unto his own, that salvation might come unto the children of men even through faith on his name.

To Jeff for teaching me so
much about faith.

—Kathleen

ISBN 13: 978-1-4621-4524-9

Published by CFI, an imprint of Cedar Fort, Inc.
2373 W. 700 S., Springville, UT 84663
Distributed by Cedar Fort, Inc., www.cedarfort.com

Cover design by Shawnda T. Craig
Cover design © 2022 Cedar Fort, Inc.

Printed in the United States of America

10 9 8 7 6 5 4 3 2 1

Printed on acid-free paper